T0003523

# THE
# WORLD
## OF THE
# FIRST
# CHRISTIANS

## A CURIOUS KID'S GUIDE TO
## THE EARLY CHURCH

BY MARC OLSON
ILLUSTRATED BY JEMIMA MAYBANK

beaming
books
MINNEAPOLIS

*For all those who hear a word that changes everything.*

*And for Sara, who rescues me from the deep holes
of historical research with fresh flowers.*

—M.O.

Text copyright © 2020 Marc Olson
Illustration copyright © 2020 Beaming Books

Published in 2020 by Beaming Books, an imprint of 1517 Media. All rights reserved.
No part of this book may be reproduced without the written permission of the publisher.
Email copyright@1517.media. Printed in China.

26 25 24 23          3 4 5 6 7 8

ISBN: 978-1-5064-6049-9

Library of Congress Cataloging-in-Publication Data
Names: Olson, Marc, 1971- author. | Maybank, Jemima, illustrator.
Title: The world of the first Christians : a curious kid's guide to the
   early church / by Marc Olson ; illustrated by Jemima Maybank.
Description: Minneapolis, MN : Beaming Books, an imprint of 1517 Media,
   2020. | Series: Curious kid's guide | Audience: Ages 5-13 | Summary:
   "The life and teachings of Jesus changed the world forever--but what
   happened after the events of the Gospels? How did Christianity grow from
   a small group of followers to one of the largest religious movements in
   human history? How did the first Christians survive in an oppressive
   Roman Empire? What did the early church believe, and how did they
   worship? The World of the First Christians: A Curious Kid's Guide to the
   Early Church answers these questions and more, with colorful
   illustrations, charts, graphs, maps, and other infographics that will
   keep kids' attention for hours and give them new insight and
   understanding into the early growth of the Christian faith. Curious
   Kids' Guides present cool and surprising information about Christian
   history and beliefs in an entertaining, visually engaging way for
   kids"-- Provided by publisher.
Identifiers: LCCN 2019050957 | ISBN 9781506460499 (hardcover)
Subjects: LCSH: Church history--Primitive and early church, ca.
   30-600--Juvenile literature. | Rome--Civilization--Juvenile literature.
   | Rome--Religious life and customs--Juvenile literature.
Classification: LCC BR165 .O44 2020 | DDC 270.1--dc23
LC record available at https://lccn.loc.gov/2019050957

Beaming Books
PO Box 1209
Minneapolis, MN 55440-1209
Beamingbooks.com

# TABLE OF CONTENTS

# INTRODUCTION

This is a book about the first people to follow Jesus and eventually call themselves Christians. They lived during the time of the Romans—one of the most powerful empires to exist in human history, and one of the most oppressive.

This book is about that time and those places, and the amazing people and things and mysteries and marvels that existed in the world that first received the news about Jesus. Using the tools of scholarship, archaeology, sociology, and history, it presents facts and insights about the people, locations, and events that surrounded the wobbly birth and wild first centuries of a people who came to be known as Christians. We call it a guide with the hope that it will help time travelers like you see the sights and understand a little bit about the first Christians and their neighbors as you explore their ancient world.

## Where Are We?

Jesus spent his whole life in the lands around Galilee and Judea in what was then a Roman province called Palestine, but the stories about his life, death, and resurrection quickly traveled beyond that place and into a much wider world. This book focuses on the lands surrounding the Mediterranean sea - a collection of nations and cities and cultures that, in the time we're exploring, formed the largest and most powerful empire the world had ever known. At its height in the year 117 CE, the Roman Empire stretched all the way from Arabia in the East to Britain in the North, and from the deserts of North Africa to the shores of the Black Sea.

## When Are We?

The most recent books of the Bible - the ones that make up what we call the New Testament, were most likely written between the years 40 and 200 CE. This book focuses on the three hundred year period between Jesus lifetime and the moment when the Christians' religion became a legal option in the Roman Empire.

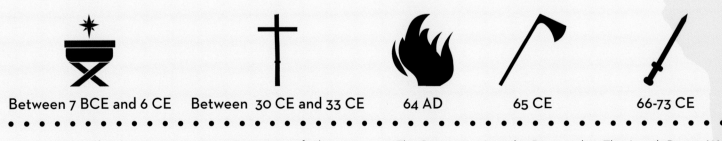

| Between 7 BCE and 6 CE | Between 30 CE and 33 CE | 64 AD | 65 CE | 66-73 CE |
|---|---|---|---|---|
| Jesus is born. | Jesus is crucified. | The Great Fire of Rome | Apostles Peter and Paul are executed | The Jewish-Roman War |

In putting this book together, we went looking for information. And here's the thing about ancient information: it can be hard to find. So this book consists of the following:

## WHAT WE KNOW
There are some documented facts about the ancient world. These come from written sources or other artifacts that have survived over the years, or have been passed along through copies. This includes the Bible, as well as all kinds of other writing.

## WHAT WE THINK WE KNOW
Based on these ancient witnesses, we make some assumptions and projections that seem to make sense. We have very likely made mistakes.

## WHAT WE KNOW WE DON'T KNOW
An awful lot.

## WHAT WE DON'T KNOW WE DON'T KNOW
Our vision of the ancient world will always be incomplete. We can't smell what the ancients smelled, or hear tones of voice, or walk in the actual shoes of our ancestors. But we can study and imagine the people who lived in these places so long ago, trusting that they'll tell us something about our own time.

## Rome, Rome, and Rome
In this book, we use the name "Rome" a lot. It's a single word that has at least two meanings.

## A City
First of all, Rome is an ancient Italian city. It was founded almost a thousand years before Jesus was born, so it was already old when the first Christians showed up in its streets and markets. Rome was home to rulers and conquerors, and, eventually, emperors. As the Roman Empire grew and spread, city dwellers all over looked to this capital city as the example or model for all cities, and often tried to imitate everything from the architecture to the fashion to the food.

## An Empire
Rome the city took up a few square miles. The empire it ruled, however, spread over two million square miles, and included more than 20% of the world's population. Sometimes when we say Rome, we mean this larger territory—and the widespread web of soldiers and governors and taxes and tributes that made it all work.

**313 CE**

The Edict of Milan makes being a Christian legal

**476 CE**

Rome falls.

# THE FIRST CHRISTIANS

The very first followers of Jesus were the same people who knew him when he traveled and healed and taught in Palestine. They were the ones who witnessed his crucifixion. After the risen Jesus appeared to some of these friends and followers, they began to worship together at the great temple in Jerusalem. They were the first believers—and the church grew from that core group.

## The Seventy

Along with the smaller group of twelve, a larger bunch of disciples had surrounded, served, and learned from Jesus while he was living. This included seventy people whom Jesus sent out into the cities and towns around Galilee to announce the arrival of God's kingdom. It's likely that many of these people were also part of the community that gathered in Jerusalem to see what would happen next. Some became deacons in the early church, charged with caring for the community's poor and vulnerable.

Thaddeus

James, son of Alphaeus

Thomas

Bartholomew

Philip

Matthew

Andrew

## LATE TO THE PARTY

A Jewish Pharisee named Saul, from the city of Tarsus, was an early enemy of the Jesus followers. After experiencing a vision of the resurrected Jesus, Saul changed his life and became an apostle. Sometime later, he became known as Paul. His work helped spread the news about Jesus throughout the world.

*"I'm the least of the apostles, because I used to persecute God's church."*

A Few of Paul's Coworkers

Timothy

Priscilla

Barnabas

Silas

Aquila

## About a Hundred and Twenty

The book of Acts says that, all told, the whole Christian movement began with about 120 people, including Jesus' mother and brothers. Jesus' brother James would become one of the most important leaders of the church in Jerusalem. Over the course of the next three hundred years, this tiny group of believers would shift and spread and grow to include millions of people.

## WHAT TO CALL THEM?

As a name to describe the followers of Jesus, the word *Christian* probably started in the Syrian city of Antioch. The local people invented a name for the strange group of people who came from all levels of society and different ethnic backgrounds, but shared Jesus-worship in common. They called them "Christians," which means Christ-followers. Mostly, the first Christian believers referred to themselves and each other as "saints" and "disciples."

## The Twelve

The small group of men whom Jesus gathered to be his disciples are known as "The Twelve." The first Christians recognized these original disciples (with Matthias replacing Judas) as the ones most qualified to lead the church and to take the message about Jesus into the wider world. They became known as "apostles," from a Greek word for "one who is sent with a mission or purpose." It has been commonly thought that the twelve apostles represented the twelve tribes of Israel. Legends about each of these guys tell where their missionary travels took them.

## And the Women!

Women had always been part of the circle around Jesus. They became leaders and teachers among the first Christians as well. Women were the first witnesses to Jesus' resurrection—even when some of his male followers refused to believe it. Mary Magdalene is known to many as the first apostle.

# LETTERS AND EPISTLES

People in the Roman Empire wrote letters for all the usual reasons: to do business, to make announcements, and to communicate with family and friends. But there was also a very different kind of letter, called an *epistle*. Epistles were long letters intended for a wide audience. They were used to teach, and they contained arguments or explanations that were useful to a whole group of people.

This type of letter became important among the Christians as a way to build relationships between churches that were separated by many miles, while also teaching the faith and supporting the new believers. Some of these letters—especially the letters of the apostle Paul—helped establish the teachings of this new religion and eventually became part of the New Testament.

## Scribes and Scrolls

Not everyone who had something to say was necessarily a good or speedy writer. Many authors in the ancient world chose to dictate their letters by speaking them aloud, and a secretary or scribe would take care of the actual writing. After the first draft was dictated, the author checked it over and made corrections. Finally, the scribe wrote out a clean, perfect, final copy.

Though the apostle Paul could certainly read and write, he used scribes and secretaries in his letter-writing work. The only one we know by name greets the Romans near the end of that letter: "I, Tertius, who wrote down this letter, greet you in the Lord" (Romans 16:22).

## Ink

Two colors of ink were in common use among the ancients. Black ink was made with lampblack (carbon residue from burning), gum arabic, and charcoal. It resisted fading and was cheap and pretty easy to make. Red ink was made with beeswax, ochre, gum, and gelatin.

## Pens

Ancient pens were made from a specific kind of reed that grew on the banks of the Nile River. A normal pen was 8-10 inches long and cut to a sharp point with a little split in the tip.

# PAUL'S LETTERS, BY LENGTH

**Romans** 7,111 words
The scroll would have been 16 1/3 feet long. In Paul's day, the papyrus alone would have cost about $600 in today's currency.

**1 Corinthians** 6,830 words
The scroll would have been slightly more than 15 feet long. $550 in papyrus.

**2 Corinthians** 4,477 words
The scroll would have been a smidge more than 10 feet long. $370 in papyrus.

**Galatians** 2,230 words
The scroll would have been slightly more than 5 feet long. $190 in papyrus.

**Philippians** 1,629 words
The scroll would have been about 3 feet long. $136 in papyrus.

**1 Thessalonians** 1,481 words
The scroll would have been 3 feet long. $127 in papyrus.

**Philemon** 335 words
The scroll would have been under a foot long, and cost about $26.50.

## Paper

Ancient writers had two main types of paper to write on: papyrus and parchment. Papyrus was made from papyrus reeds, which were flattened into sheets and then glued together to make scrolls. Parchment was made with animal hides, and was more durable than papyrus. Sheets of parchment were sewn rather than glued to make scrolls.

# THE GOSPEL AND ITS GOSPELS

The word *gospel* (in Greek it's *euangelion*) had a life before the first Christians started using it to talk about Jesus. The word, which means "good news" or "glad tidings" or (loosely translated) "awesome sauce," had been part of the Greek language for centuries. Early uses included announcing the end of war and arrival of peace brought about by a king's victory. In the days of the Roman Empire it was often used as a way to honor and celebrate the emperor. Is your city getting a visit from the royal retinue? That was announced as "Good News!" Have you been promoted to a higher office in the government? "Glad Tidings!" Has the emperor decided to pay for a month of gladiatorial games and toss in free bread for all the inhabitants of your town? "Awesome Sauce!"

## FOUR STORIES

During the decades after Jesus' resurrection, all kinds of gospels were written. Four seemed to become the best loved and most widely shared. We know them as Matthew, Mark, Luke, and John, even though most agree that those are not likely the names of their original authors. Each was written with a specific audience in mind, and as these accounts spread, churches realized what a gift they were—even in their differences. Along with Paul's letters, the four gospels were among the earliest writings to be treasured as holy scripture by the first Christians.

### MATTHEW

**Written around 90 AD**
**Maybe in Antioch, Syria**

- "You are the light of the world!"

- To the Jewish people: Jesus is the one you've been waiting for—surprise!

- He's God's Messiah! He fulfills all the scriptures! Let's follow him.

### MARK

**Written around 70 AD**
**Maybe in Palestine**

- "Look at all the amazing stuff he does!"

- The Son of God came to be with you, and to heal and save you— even if you're too poor to follow all God's laws. Jesus changes everything! Sinners welcome!

## The Gospel Becomes the Gospels

The first Christians learned early on that the good news about Jesus' resurrection was best understood when shared along with the whole story of his life and death—especially as the Christian message moved further away from the places where and the people among whom Jesus had lived and worked. Anonymous preachers, writers, missionaries, and storytellers added to the apostles' and disciples' accounts of their master's sayings and miracles, relating fuller versions of Jesus' life story. After a while, these started to be written down and shared, and a new type of literature was born: the Christian gospel.

**"I did the gospel thing before any of these guys!"**

Even though his writing did not include the story of Jesus' life, death, and resurrection, Paul the evangelist wrote letters full of gospel news. His letters were in circulation as early as 55 AD, and he died before the first of the gospels (Mark) was written. Paul uses the word *euangelion* more than any other writer in the Bible—more than eighty times.

## The Gospel of Augustus

One ancient pronouncement, celebrating the reign of the emperor Augustus, describes how he was sent to the people as "savior and god," and how this was and is "good news [*euangelion*] for all humanity." This message was carved in stone and set up in the Greek coastal city of Priene in 9 BC. The good news Christians brought to the Roman world was a response to that kind of good news: they were saying that Jesus, and not the emperor, was the real savior of humanity.

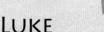

### LUKE

**Written around 90 AD, but probably after Matthew Maybe in Ephesus**

• "I'm trustworthy, and so is Jesus."

• Jesus opens God's promises to all people—even Greeks and Romans!

• He is wise and good, and totally worth worshipping.

• I also wrote the Acts of the Apostles. Trust me—I was there!

### JOHN

**Written around 90–100 AD Probably in Asia Minor**

• "It's gonna be OK!"

• Hold on, Christians! To see God, look at Jesus. In Jesus, you can see that God loves you so much! Now follow Jesus by loving each other.

# MOVING THE MAIL

Letters were hugely important to the Roman Empire. A letter could carry detailed and specific orders or announcements from a military or government official across the empire in every direction. Rome even had a postal service for official communications called the *cursus publicus*. Messengers on horseback, exchanging tired horses for fresh ones every few hours, could travel more than 150 miles in a single day and night.

The super-speedy *cursus publicus* was reserved for the official business of the empire. Everyone else had to make do with private couriers, who charged a fee to deliver letters; friends or even strangers who were headed in the direction you wanted your letter to go.

The Roman god Mercury, like the Greeks' Hermes, is known as the messenger of the gods and the patron of letter carriers. He is often pictured with winged sandals and a winged cap.

A good courier had to be physically fit, smart, resourceful, brave, and loyal. They had to be literate as well. Sometimes the courier was also expected to read the letter on arrival—and answer questions. Often, the courier would stick around while a response was written, and then carry that letter back to the original sender.

## Some Letter Carriers of the New Testament

- **Phoebe**, *a church leader and deacon from a town near Corinth.* Phoebe had friends and connections among the Roman churches, so she was the perfect person to carry and share Paul's longest letter.

- **Timothy**, *Paul's closest assistant and friend.* Timothy helped Paul write several letters and carried messages to and from both the Thessalonians and the Corinthians.

- **Titus**, *another of Paul's close associates and trusted friends.* Titus carried messages to the Corinthians and other churches in Macedonia and Asia.

- **Epaphroditus**, *a member of the church at Philippi.* He brought gifts and messages back and forth between his community and Paul's team. According to Paul's note about him in the letter to the Philippians, Epaphroditus almost died on his journey.

- **Onesimus**, *a slave who either ran away or was dismissed from the house of Philemon, a church leader among the Colossians.* Onesimus carried Paul's letter that urged Philemon to take him back, no longer as a slave but as a brother.

## LETTERS FROM PAUL

Among the Christians, the most prolific letter writer we know about was the apostle Paul. Paul's letters were usually carried by a trustworthy courier who could also read and explain the letter's content. Sometimes that person was a member of the community the letter was going to. Sometimes the courier was part of Paul's trusted team.

## Maybe Send a Couple

Every journey was risky. Even on the well-maintained Roman roads, bad weather or bandits could slow a courier down or steal what they carried. Ships sank or were delayed by storms. And couriers could get sick or hurt or distracted, or might take other jobs from people who paid better. One ancient letter was delayed by nine years! Facing so many possible disasters, sometimes the letter writer sent two copies, with two different couriers.

# BAPTISM

The Greek word for baptism is basically the same word that got used to describe dipping or bathing—even washing dishes. To be baptized was, essentially, to be rinsed with water. Religious baptism is based on the idea that getting the body clean with a bath can announce and embody a new spiritual start.

Christians have been baptizing since the earliest days. The New Testament, which uses the word more than 120 times, includes Jesus himself sending his followers and friends into the world to baptize others, "teaching them to obey everything I have commanded you" (Matthew 28:20). There's good reason to believe that wherever there were Christians, there was some baptizing going on.

Like the birth of a longed-for baby, baptisms were reasons for the community of Christians to celebrate. The church welcomed its new members out of the water, clothing them in a clean, new robe and celebrating with songs and hugs and kisses.

## It Took Two

Other religions in the ancient world also had ritual washing, but some of those ceremonies were self-administered. Christian baptism was different because it required at least two people: one to do the dunking or pouring and to speak the words, and the other to let it all happen to them. Often, a larger group was present to help welcome the newly baptized into the full life of the church, the family of God. This included the Eucharist meal, which usually happened very soon after a baptism.

## A Big Deal

Among the Christians, baptism was no small matter. Just like birth, baptism signified a once-for-all-time passage from one identity to a whole new identity—being "in Christ" and partaking in God's Spirit. The salvation of baptism included forgiveness of sins, a new start, and a transfer from death to eternal life. The apostle Paul described baptism as being buried and raised with Christ. Candidates for baptism learned these things as part of their preparation, which included prayer and fasting.

Christian life after baptism was a big deal too. Just as it connected the baptized to Christ and the community of sisters and brothers, baptism also separated the new believer from the wider community of nonbelievers, sometimes including networks of friends and family. Claiming and confessing Jesus as Lord meant denying that title to anyone else—including the emperor and the gods of Rome.

Because they had no buildings specifically dedicated to the ceremony, the first Christians, like their model baptizer John, used whatever body of water they had access to. Usually this was a river, stream, lake, or pond.

## Not Just Water

Getting wet was the visible part of baptism. Just as important as this outward sign were the words spoken along with the washing. The first Christians often baptized in the name of Jesus; by the time the gospels were written down, most baptisms were celebrated in the name of the Father, the Son, and the Holy Spirit, along with a threefold plunge or sprinkle. This was followed by laying on of hands and a prayer for the presence and blessing of the Holy Spirit.

# ROME AND ITS CITIES

By the middle of the second century, nearly one out of every three people in the Roman Empire lived in a city. There were about 1,500 cities scattered throughout the empire. Most were fairly small, with populations of 10,000 to 15,000 people, but cities like Alexandria, Ephesus, and Carthage had hundreds of thousands of residents. Rome itself was the biggest city in the world. By the year 160, as many as a million people called Rome home.

On the street level of the *insulae*, merchants and artisans had workshops and storefronts. City streets were paved with stone and often had raised sidewalks, which also served as front steps for the shops. As well as being the place to buy items like clothing, fabric, pottery, jewelry, or metal items, street-side shops were gathering places for friends or acquaintances. Out-of-towners could stop on the street to get directions or make connections.

## Getting a Lift Downtown

Roman city streets were noisy and crowded with all manner of humanity, not to mention garbage, poop, and even dead animals. When the wealthy wanted to move about town, they sometimes rode in *litters* to float above it all. A litter was a platform or covered compartment fitted with handles so it could be carried by four or more people. It was like a carriage, but with slaves or hired porters instead of wheels.

Large tenement buildings, called *insulae* ("islands") because each one took up an entire city block, stood as high as six or seven stories. Most of the urban population lived in these structures, typically in dark and crowded apartments without kitchen or bathroom facilities. The best and most expensive apartments were on the lower floors. The smallest and most cramped quarters were right under the tile roofs, reachable only by climbing lots of stairs. Rome included thousands of these big buildings. Most were cheaply made of timber and bricks, and were owned by landlords who cared little about safety. At best, insulae were drafty and leaky; at worst, they collapsed or caught fire, with disastrous results.

Romans liked dogs. While most city canines were kept as watchdogs, some enjoyed life as family pets and companions. In the countryside, some people kept hunting and herding dogs. Some Roman dogs even wore collars with their owner's name on them. This Latin sign says "Beware of Dog."

CAVE CANEM

Priscilla and Aquila, leaders among the first Christians, made their living as tentmakers in the city of Rome, and then in Corinth. Their workshops in these cities would very likely have been on the ground floor of an *insula*, with a living area upstairs. Paul lived and worked with Priscilla and Aquila in Corinth for over a year, sewing leather tents while talking about Jesus and drafting letters together. Their shop would have been a meeting place for local Christians as well as visitors.

## Water Makes It Happen

Fresh water for public baths and fountains, as well as for use in the homes of the wealthy, was brought into the city using aqueducts. Built like bridges using stone and concrete, some aqueducts ran for miles, connecting the city to a source of fresh water, usually a spring or perennial stream in nearby hills or mountains.

# ROME AND ITS CITIES, CONT.

Most business and commerce in a Roman city happened early in the day; the streets would be full of shoppers, slaves, messengers, and delivery-persons during the morning. In the afternoon the wealthier classes spent time visiting the bath or gymnasium, as well as socializing. Slaves and most other workers kept whatever hours their masters and employers dictated. Most people rose with the sun, so bedtime was often early.

To protect property from thieves and burglars, most houses didn't have ground-level windows facing the street. If they did, the windows usually had iron bars.

## Grab a Snack

Though they didn't have drive-through service or intercoms through which you could shout your order, Roman towns and cities were filled with popular walk-up restaurants or taverns, called *thermopolia* (literally, "places where hot is sold"). A *thermopolium* often had a counter or bar that was open to the street. Patrons stepped right up and ordered food—like baked cheese with honey, or a cup of hot stew, ladled from a jar set right into the countertop. All kinds and classes of people ate this fast food—sometimes as an on-the-go snack or a main meal. Some ate standing or walked off while nibbling their treat. Others found a place to sit in a side room of the establishment. Among the poor, whose apartments included no spot for cooking, *thermopolia* were a way to get a cheap and easy hot meal.

**Law and Order**
One of the first acts of Emperor Augustus was to create a Roman police force called the Urban Cohorts. Unlike the police as we know them, who respond to crime calls and conduct investigations, these semi-soldiers were on hand to keep order and put down riots or rebellions. Augustus also created a group called the Vigiles Urbani. These people served as firefighters and night watchmen in Rome. Other large cities in the empire followed Rome's example and organized Vigiles and Urban Cohorts of their own.

# Get a Trim

Ancient Romans were careful about their looks. This included the clothes they wore, as well as how their hair and faces looked and smelled. Working on the street or in barbershops (*tonstrinae*), a barber (*tonsor*) shaved his clients with bronze razors sharpened with stones, or yanked out the hairs with beeswax and tweezers. Barbers also offered head massages, haircuts, nose hair service, fingernail trimming, and even the occasional tooth extraction! Roman men spent long hours in the barbershop, socializing, trading news and gossip, and perfecting their look. Men and women with higher social rank and more money had their own barbers and hairdressers among their slaves.

# DINNER IN PHILIPPI 50 CE

In the book of Acts, the apostle Paul, along with his companions Silas and Timothy, find themselves in the Roman colonial city of Philippi. It doesn't take them long to meet a local businesswoman named Lydia, a trader in expensive purple-dyed cloth. Lydia is, apparently, the first person in town to be baptized. She then hosts Paul and his friends at her house and, we can presume, introduces them to her network of friends, hired workers, clients, and contacts. One of the best ways to do this in the ancient world (as in today's) was by having a dinner party.

We don't know, of course, what she served or exactly who was there, but Lydia would have treated her guests much like any other wealthy householder at the time, following customs and codes that made sure everyone and everything had a proper place.

## A Meal in Three Movements

A Roman dinner consisted of three parts: the *gustus*, or appetizer; the *cena*, or dinner proper; and the *secunda mensa*—dessert (literally, the "second table").

- The *gustus* could include spiced shellfish, uncooked onions, olives, pickles, and eggs. Stuffed, roasted dormice were a regular treat throughout the empire, but especially in the northern parts. These roasted rodents might have been dipped in honey or stuffed with meat and pine nuts.

- The *cena*, or main course, might include asparagus and mushrooms as well as beans, cauliflower, and more olives. Warm loaves of bread were on hand. Meats like goat, pork, or fish were the typical main dish—sometimes even a whole roast boar, wreathed in rosemary.

- A sweet, salty, funky sauce called *garum* was part of nearly every meal in the ancient empire. It was made of heavily salted and chopped-up fish leftovers, like heads, fins, and guts. Large clay pots of this pungent goop fermented in the hot Mediterranean sun for nine months before it was ready to eat. The sauce was so stinky that it was against the law to make it within city limits. But everybody loved it.

- Finally, dessert was served. This *secunda mensa* could feature honey-sweetened pastries, walnuts, peaches, cherries, apples, or even snails. This is also when wine flowed freely.

## Who Was Lydia?

We don't know much about Lydia, other than that she was a business owner, which would have earned her respect and status in the community, and was in charge of her own home. It's likely she was able to do these things independent of an in-charge male (or *kyrios*, "lord") because she was both a widow and a mother. During the first century, free Roman women who had borne three or four children were able to conduct business, own slaves, sign contracts, and testify in court. She wouldn't have been the only such woman in Philippi.

Women like Lydia were important members of the first Christian communities. They offered leadership as well as financial and material support to missionaries like Paul, Timothy, and Silas, and they opened their homes to the growing churches in Europe and Asia Minor. Many believe that the first church building built in Philippi was near the place where Lydia lived.

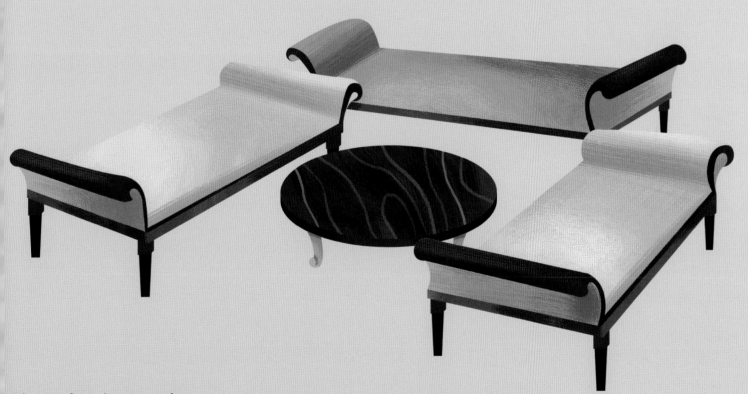

## Places for the People

A Roman dining room was set up to host nine people, separated onto three benches or couches set along three sides of a low table. The open side of the table was for serving and clearing the dishes as the meal progressed. Diners didn't sit on the couches, but reclined, leaning forward toward the table and resting on their left arm. Leaning in like this, they had the food within easy reach, and everybody's head was close enough for conversation.

If you were lucky enough to be invited to this kind of dinner, your place on the dining couch would let you know exactly where you stood (or reclined!) in terms of status. Each of the nine places at the table had a level of honor associated with it. The highest place, reserved for the guest of honor, was immediately to the left of the host.

# THE PUBLIC TOILET

Roman cities were busy and crowded places. Streets, temples, theaters, and baths were full of people: citizens and slaves, women and men, merchants and shoppers. And as anyone knows, everybody poops. Just like modern towns, ancient cities somehow had to accommodate this universal human need. In the Roman world, one answer was the public latrine.

Often located near markets, theaters, and the huge tenement apartment buildings where the majority of the city's people lived, Roman public toilets had seating for one or two dozen people at a time. The largest had room for as many as forty-five to sixty simultaneous users. And forget about privacy. The holes were placed about two feet apart, with no partitions between seats. Most of these places were poorly lit, dirty, crowded, stinky, and even a little scary.

## What about Just Holding It until You Got Home?
Nice try. Unless you were part of the wealthier classes, you were stuck with the communal public latrine. Larger homes had private facilities. Often, these were located in the kitchen so cooks could toss kitchen scraps into the hole. Some ancient apartments had a toilet on the second floor. Home toilets were rarely connected to the city sewer system; the waste just fell into a pit.

Some ancient latrines also featured a statue or wall painting of the good-luck goddess, Fortuna. It was hoped that she would help protect users from some of the dangers that inhabited these dark, smelly spaces. Such dangers included rats, mice, snakes, fleas, mosquitos, and the occasional small fire caused by methane gas buildup.

## NO SUCH THING AS TOILET PAPER

Latrine users who wanted to freshen up may have used a variety of techniques. One popular tool was the *tersorium*, a wooden stick with a sea sponge tied onto the end. Latrines would have a few of these for public use, soaking in buckets of salt water or vinegar. While this may have been an okay way to feel a little cleaner, we know now that it was a really good way to spread sickness and disease.

Roman toilets didn't flush. Sometimes, there may have been a trickle of water in the space below the seats, but this was rarely enough to carry things away. The task of cleaning out sewer pipes, as well as cleaning up the public latrines, most likely fell to a city's slaves. Human waste from the sewers, along with other street sweepings and bio-waste, was often carted outside the city, where it could be used as fertilizer for growing food crops.

# THE ARENA

What we call the Colosseum, in the heart of Rome, was known in its time as the Flavian Amphitheater, but most people likely called it "the arena." What happened in the arena was a mixture of professional sports, theatrical entertainment, brutal justice, and bloody cruelty. The ground-floor arches were entrance and exit gates. The arches on the second and third levels each held statues depicting the various gods and virtues.

## WEAPONS USED BY GLADIATORS

A. Gladius (sword)
B. Sica
C. Net
D. Pugio dagger
E. Trident
F. Arcus (Bow) and Sagitta (Arrow)

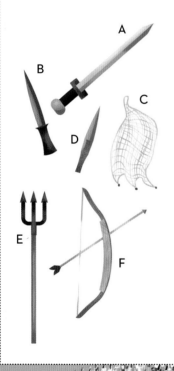

The Flavian Amphitheater could hold more than 50,000 people.

The floor of the arena was made of wooden planks covered by a layer of sand. Beneath that floor was a labyrinth of ramps, passages, animal pens, holding cells, and storage rooms. Trap doors in the floor could be opened to release animals into the arena, or to make it look like a gladiator appeared from nowhere.

Some historians believe the entire floor of the arena could be flooded with water for the reenactment of famous naval battles.

## Among the Christians

Though we have no way of knowing who came and went through the arches of the amphitheater, the Christians were not fans of the arena and its entertainments. Persecution of Christians over the decades resulted in Christians being executed in the arena. Some Christians died in the teeth of wild animals, or beneath merciless

Arena crowds gathered to watch well-trained gladiators fight each other to the death, and to witness the hunting or fighting of wild animals, including bears, lions, giraffes, wild boars, rhinoceroses, crocodiles, and elephants. Another favorite spectacle included reenacting famous Roman military victories, in which the Roman army would be played by gladiators and the enemies would be played by war prisoners or criminals. Also included were the occasional executions of criminals and traitors—especially slaves and people of the lowest social classes.

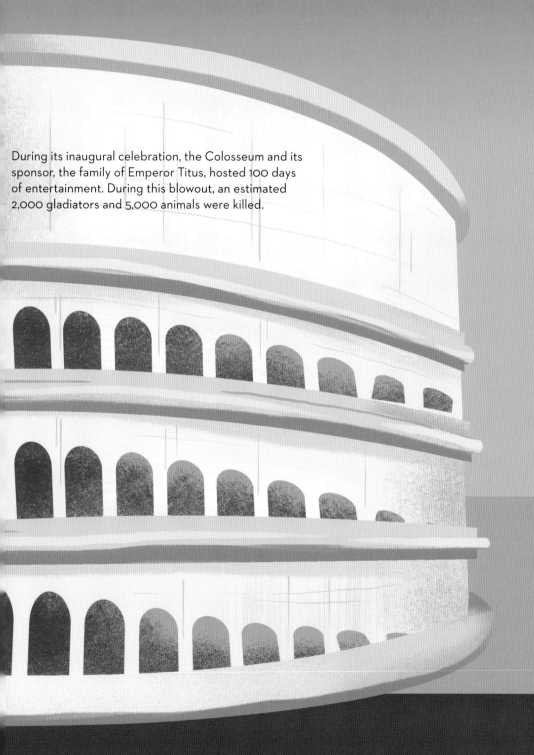

During its inaugural celebration, the Colosseum and its sponsor, the family of Emperor Titus, hosted 100 days of entertainment. During this blowout, an estimated 2,000 gladiators and 5,000 animals were killed.

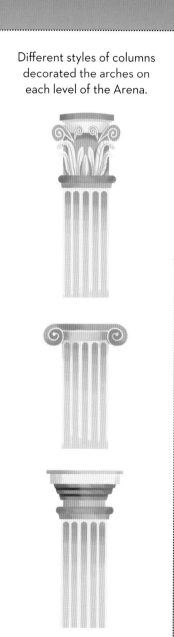

Different styles of columns decorated the arches on each level of the Arena.

swords, among the cheers and jeers of the masses. This gave later Christians even more of a reason to hate the games and their brutality.

# THE GLADIATORS

The Romans valued bravery and brute strength. It's no wonder they loved the gladiatorial games, which allowed them to celebrate and revel in both. The word *gladiator* comes from *gladius*, the Latin word for the short, wide sword that every Roman soldier wore on his belt. The gladiators were literally "sword-men." Their job was to earn glory and honor for themselves and the powerful people who owned them by fighting to the death before crowds of thousands cheering in the arenas of Rome.

**Thraex**
*"The Thracian"*
- Head of a Griffin
- Short shield
- Curved blade

**Retiarius**
*"The Netman"*
- No helmet
- Trident
- Weighted net

**Summa Rudis**
*"The Referee"*
- Longstaff

**Eques**
*"The Horseman"*
- Helmet with two feathers
- Tunic
- Round shield
- Long sword
- Padded shin protectors

**Murmillo**
*"The Fish"*
- Gladus sword
- Rectangular shield
- Short shin guard

Gladiators were usually slaves, prisoners of war from the nations conquered by Rome, or criminals, condemned to fight for their lives. Occasionally, a free person or former soldier volunteered to become a gladiator for the excitement, fame, and fortune that might be involved, but this was rare.

Gladiator combat was part theatre and part sport. A gladiator was dressed and equipped as a specific type of character—usually representing Rome's soldiers or their historical enemies. His weapons and armor showed the crowd which character he was. Different gladiator types were pitted against each other.

## Provocator
### *"The Attacker"*

Rectangular shield

Chest plate

## Hoplomachus
### *"The Greek Warrior"*

Arm pads

## Secutor
### *"The Pursuer"*

No crown on his helmet

Arm protector

Long spear

Small round shield

Shin guards

## LIFE IN THE *LUDUS*

- Gladiator trainees practiced fighting every day, under the eye of a training master and manager called the *lanista*. They wrestled and boxed, and sparred with blunt or wooden weapons so nobody would get badly hurt. Gladiators were fed a strictly vegetarian diet, bathed regularly, and were attended by physicians who kept them healthy.

- A well-trained gladiator with good skills might be able to fight and win for years, even earning enough glory and money to purchase his freedom. A freed gladiator was given a wooden sword, called a *rudis*, as a symbol of his freedom. Some freed gladiators kept fighting for the sake of money and fame; others became trainers.

- Before a gladiator could even think of earning his freedom, he had to fight. And he had to win. And that means somebody else had to lose. Historians estimate the life expectancy of a Roman gladiator to have been around twenty-seven years old.

# ROADS

By the time the Roman Empire reached its peak around the year 120 AD, the Romans had built more than 50,000 miles of roads. These were not simple trails. The engineered and paved roads that connected the cities of the empire were so sturdy and amazing that some are still in use today. Like the mail, Roman roads helped Christianity spread quickly, as missionaries could carry the message of Jesus from city to city.

Roman roads reached from the banks of the Euphrates River all the way to the middle of England and to the western coast of Spain.

If Rome was the heart of the empire, the roads were the blood vessels. They connected cities to other cities, and big cities to their closest seaports. Most cargo and trade goods traveled by ship, though large ox-drawn freight wagons, called *plaustra*, rumbled along the roads, often passed by travelers riding speedier chariots or trotting horses. A courier on official government business could travel as many as 75 miles in a single day, changing horses at well-placed way stations. People without animals to ride, or money to pay for a carriage ride, walked the edges of these roads.

Along the major roads, builders placed large cylindrical milestones to let travelers know exactly where they were. These columns listed the distance in miles to the central forum in the city of Rome.

- As engineers and builders, the Romans were in a class by themselves. They built bridges, carved tunnels, and drained swamps to overcome obstacles. The Romans also invented concrete, made from a cement mixed up with volcanic ash and crushed limestone.

  The original reason for all this amazing building activity was to move large numbers of soldiers as quickly as possible from one place to another. On a smooth, straight road, troops could march 15 or 20 miles in a day and still be fresh enough to fight when they arrived.

- Known to the Romans as the regina viarum, or "Queen of Roads," the Appian Way was one of the first of the long Roman roads. This road stretched approximately 100 miles and was later elongated an additional 230+ miles to reach all the way to the Adriatic seaport of Brindisi.

- The apostle Paul and countless other Christians would have walked the Roman roads. Some, like Paul, made it a mission to carry the news about Jesus to places best reached by the roads of Rome. One estimate is that Paul walked as many as 10,000 miles between the time he began his ministry and his eventual end in Rome.

# TRAVEL ON THE "WET WAY"

By the time the first Christians were boarding boats to ports across the Roman Empire, sailors of many nations had been piloting various crafts on the Mediterranean Sea for more than two thousand years. The most well-traveled routes stayed close to the shoreline, moving goods and people between port cities. Ancient sailors also had the skills and knowledge that allowed them to venture beyond the sight of land in all directions.

Clay vessels called *amphorae* were ancient shipping containers. Ships were outfitted with racks to hold the amphorae, which were filled with wine or olive oil, or grains such as wheat. Often the amphorae were sealed with wet clay that was stamped with a label describing the contents and source. The largest Roman cargo ships could carry tens of thousands of amphorae in one load.

Even if there weren't hills to climb or bandits to avoid, seafaring had its share of danger. With heavy loads and only simple sails, merchant ships were prone to sink in bad weather. Shipwrecks were common during the stormy seasons of the Mediterranean.

For an amazing account of a first-century storm and shipwreck near the Mediterranean island of Malta, read the 27th chapter of Acts.

Some ships, called galleys, relied on teams of rowers to move across the water. Galleys could travel even when the winds were still, and they could turn and maneuver in ways that sailing craft could not. They were most often used for warfare or other official imperial business.

Merchant ships sacrificed the advantages of oar power for the sake of space for stuff. If warships were long and narrow, cargo haulers were tall and round, and depended on their sails for power. Some of the ships that moved goods around the empire could carry up to 400 tons of cargo. Manned by a crew of ten or twelve, these big boats carried news, information, and passengers as well as cargo—which could include everything from wheat, oil, and lumber to gold and exotic animals.

Nearly all the ships that moved on the first-century Mediterranean had at least one big, square sail, set in the middle of the ship.

## THE MEDITERRANEAN SEA

- Because the Mediterranean was the center of the Roman world, and the heart that kept grain flowing from all corners of the empire to the capital city of Rome, Romans called it *Mare Nostrum*, which means "our sea."

- The Mediterranean Sea averages almost a mile deep, with the deepest parts over 17,000 feet.

- The Mediterranean Sea touches the coasts of three continents: Asia, Africa (which the Romans called Libya), and Europe. With hundreds of known and well-traveled sea routes, the Mediterranean connected these diverse places in a web of communication, trade, and common culture. The first Christians brought the message about Jesus on board various sailing vessels and carried it wherever the wind blew.

# THE FIRST CHRISTIAN SYMBOLS

Symbols are ways people communicate meaning with simple signs or pictures. In the earliest years of the Jesus movement, Christians chose to mark their worship spaces and monuments with a handful of images and words that told the story of their faith, and offered a vision of how they claimed and celebrated life in Jesus. And in times of persecution, these symbols allowed Christians to share their faith with each other without others knowing what the symbols meant.

Like the crossbar of an anchor, a ship's mast was also a place Christians saw the cross. Some Christian ship images also include a dove perched along the beam, with a branch in its mouth.

Some have suggested that these anchor images also contain the cross—a way for Christians to see their own important meaning in the more familiar sign.

## ANCHORED IN HOPE

Some Christians marked gravestones with anchors. The anchor was an image of hope and stability in the middle of what was for many people a stormy and unpredictable life. Writing in the second half of the first century, the author of the letter to the Hebrews uses the image of an anchor to describe Christian hope in Christ (Hebrews 6:19-20).

## FISH, FOOD, AND
## THE BASICS OF FAITH

In Greek, the word for "fish," Ichthys, contains five letters: *I - ch - th - y - s*. At some point in the first century, some clever Christian noticed that these letters together told the basic story at the heart of the new faith. I stood for "Jesus," ch stood for "Christ," th stood for "God" (*theos*, in Greek), y stood for "Son" (*yios*, in Greek), and s stood for "Savior" (*soter*, in Greek). The first Christians found, crammed into this simple and common word, a shorthand way of teaching, learning, and remembering the basic confession of faith.

## Where Are All the Crosses?

Though the cross is hidden in many of these symbols—the anchor, the ship's mast, and the letter symbols—early Christians didn't use the cross by itself as a symbol.

Crucifixion was a punishment for traitors, bandits, murderers, and slaves. It took a while for Christians to make up their own minds about how they felt about Jesus' execution on a cross—and what that cross meant and how to describe it. Within a century or so, the cross was to become the most important and most recognizable symbol of Christianity, but it wasn't the first.

## SAFE PASSAGE

Early Christians also used the image of a ship to describe and celebrate the experience of faith. The Bible's story of Noah's ark describes a small group of humans and other creatures being saved from the destruction of God's judgment. The first Christians understood the church to be in the same boat (so to speak)—a people gathered by Christ into an ark of safety. The inside were protected from the chaos and storms of life.

## LETTERS

Some of the first Christian symbols were simply arrangements of the Greek letters in Jesus' name or title. One symbol, called the chi-rho, is simply the first two letters of the Greek word "Christ" stacked on top of each other. Two other letter-symbols that were common among the early Christians are the first and last letters of the Greek alphabet, alpha and omega—because Jesus said he was "the Alpha and the Omega, the beginning and the end" (Revelation 21:6).

# PROTECTIVE MAGIC

In the ancient world, medicine, magic, and religion were all blended together in people's minds. Amulets were objects made by specialists intended to capture and use the power of the spirits and gods to protect the wearer from all kinds of harm.

A magic amulet could be made from almost anything. Materials used included bone, metal, glass, animal hide, papyrus, stone, clay, cloth, string, and wood. Rarer materials included gold, silver, gemstones, and crystals.

For a price, a magician would make amulets that supposedly helped with love, charms to attract good luck and blessings, and jewelry intended to ward off evil spirits or the envious curses of enemies. These all had their uses, but by far the most common type of magic charm had to do with health.

Before the invention of modern medicine, sanitation, and refrigerated food storage, illness was common—especially in big cities, where people lived close together. Mysterious fevers were frequent, as were digestive problems, infections, ear and toothaches, and coughs. In addition to rest and other remedies, people used magic to take care of illnesses.

An amulet to treat a fever might include a few magic words written on a strip of paper, which was then rolled and kept in a tiny wooden or glass tube on a string around the patient's neck. When the fever passed, the one-time-use charm was thrown away. Chronic illnesses, like stomachaches or difficulty breathing, required more powerful, longer-lasting magic—perhaps a gem or crystal inscribed with what the patient hoped for. One second-century Roman amulet just contained the words "Digest. Digest. Digest."

Some amulets were made in the shape of the affected body part, like a foot or hand or ear. Charms in the shape of eyes were thought to ward off the evil and envious glances of someone who might wish to harm the wearer.

Sometimes a spell or charm was stamped or engraved on a strip of precious metal and rolled up to be carried around in a wooden tube or cloth pouch. These strips were called *lamellae*.

Many Roman boy babies were given an amulet, called a *bulla*, nine days after their birth. These were meant to protect the wearer from evil spirits and to promote good health and growth to manhood.

Some amulets found in Egypt, where the dry desert helps preserve fragile papyrus, contained small passages from the gospels—especially the opening lines of the Gospel of John, or references to Jesus' healing miracles.

Christian writers generally frowned on placing faith in magic objects or dealing with spirits. Because the allure of protective magic was hard to resist, one writer counseled the faithful instead to pray the psalms when they were sick, make the sign of the cross, and be anointed with holy oil or water as a reminder that God was with them.

Later Christians wore and used the cross as protection from demons and other evils. As a wearable symbol, the cross didn't come on the scene until the fourth century, when it became more popular (and legal) to be known as a Christian.

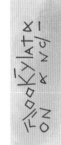

## Magic Words

One ancient physician, writing in the third century, recommended that those suffering from what we now call malaria could be cured by wearing a charm that included the word *ABRACADABRA* written in a triangle. Ancient Christians sometimes used the Hebrew word *Amen* as a charm against disease or danger.

## Among the Christians

As the Christian faith found its way across the empire, so did the name of Jesus and stories of his miracle-making power. Amulet makers used whatever they thought would work best for their charms and amulets—including words and images from this new religion.

# WHICH GOD TO WORSHIP?

Rome's empire stretched across the known world, from the Atlantic coast in the west to the plains of Mesopotamia in the east. Every nation conquered by the empire brought their own gods and religious beliefs into the Roman world, leaving people with a decision: Which god should they worship?

### Artemis of the Ephesians
**The Great Mother Goddess**

Artemis was hugely popular in the ancient world. Her temple, on a high hill in the city of Ephesus (now part of Turkey), was one of the largest buildings in the world and a place of refuge for people seeking safety and asylum. Artemis was called "the great mother goddess." She was believed to ensure fertility of all kinds: for animals and plants, as well as human beings. One legend claims she was the midwife who delivered the baby who became Alexander the Great.

Copies of the statue of Artemis of the Ephesians were found all over the ancient world. Known also as "The Lady of the Animals," her skirt was decorated with images of lions and bees. All those round things hanging around her neck are thought to represent the testicles of bulls and stallions that were sacrificed in her temple by the hundreds.

Every place struck by lightning was thought to be claimed by Jupiter.

### Jupiter
**Also known as *Iuppiter Optimus Maximus* (the Best and Biggest)**

Known as "The Light Bringer" and the god of lightning and thunder, Jupiter was the chief Roman and Italian god. Patterned after the Greek god Zeus, Jupiter was considered the father of all the other gods and the personal protective deity of the reigning Roman emperor. Jupiter was known as the god who kept worshippers in the paths of duty and loyalty to the gods, the state, and the family.

## Mithras
### The Unconquered Sun (*Sol Invictus*)

Mithras, or Mithra, was a Persian god, known as the deity of the sun, justice, and war. Mithra worship flourished in the first through the fourth centuries. As the god of friendship and mutual loyalty as well, Mithras was especially popular among soldiers who worked and lived together constantly. It's possible that Mithra worship, and its secret initiation rites, were carried throughout the empire by Roman legionaires, who encountered it while stationed in the East. Mithra worship was encouraged by military leaders and emperors because it promoted and emphasized loyalty.

Mithras is often pictured slaying a huge bull with a knife. Legend also has it that he was born out of a rock.

## Isis-Fortuna
### Queen of Heaven and Mistress of Magic

Though Isis worship originated in Egypt, she became revered throughout the empire as a patron goddess of mourners, healing, resurrection, and motherhood. As the goddess of good fortune, Isis was also very popular as a protector of sailors and seafarers, who sailed cargo ships full of wheat from Egypt and North Africa to the hungry cities of Europe. Across the empire, Isis became immensely popular among lower classes, including slaves and women.

Isis, the giver of abundant gifts, holds a cornucopia in one hand and a ship's rudder in the other. Isis was believed to have the power of life and death—and of life over death. Her magic was thought to be so powerful that it could even cheat fate. Many people had small statues and shrines to Isis in their homes.

# BABIES

Rome could be a dangerous world for babies. Historians estimate that about one quarter of the babies born didn't live to see their first birthday, and fully half of all Roman kids never made it to their tenth. While wealthy families could welcome the birth of babies, and even had servants to care for them, most regular families in the ancient world were not as fortunate.

Faced with the choice between starving with a big family and surviving with a smaller one, some chose to give away, sell, or even abandon newborn children. Even though many people thought it was immoral, child abandonment was, sadly, a not-uncommon reality and practice in the cities of the empire. It wasn't outlawed until the year 374.

Christians were different. They believed that babies were made by a God who cared for the life of each creature—and whose divine commandments outlawed murder. Christians also understood themselves as children who had been saved from death and destruction by a loving Redeemer and adopted into the family of Christ. They remembered stories about Jesus welcoming children, and often found or made room in their households and communities for orphans and foundlings.

Ancient legends are full of abandoned babies who were remarkably rescued. Romulus and Remus, the legendary heroes who founded the city of Rome, were found and nursed by a she-wolf and raised by a shepherd. Other famous foundlings included Oedipus, the Greek king, and the Jewish prophet and patriarch Moses, who was set adrift in a basket on the Nile.

Unwanted babies were sometimes placed in boxes or clay jars and set in the street, along roadways, or atop garbage heaps outside the city. Romans believed there was always a chance that the gods would intervene (in the form of a stranger or some other saving action) and take care of the child. And if it died, well, that was seen as the will of the gods too.

One Roman ritual around birth required the midwife to lay each newborn baby on the ground before the *paterfamilias*, or oldest male in the household. If he picked up the child, it became an acknowledged part of the family. If he refused, it could be abandoned. Babies could be rejected if they were unhealthy or deformed, the wrong sex, or suspected of being illegitimate.

## We Should Be at Least as Good as the Birds

One Christian writer, arguing that abandoning babies was against nature as well as immoral, pointed to the behavior of birds, who not only care for the babies that hatch from their own eggs but are known to feed and tend other birds' babies as well.

# CHURCH

Temples were plentiful in the world of the first Christians. Big cities like Rome, Alexandria, Athens, and Carthage were absolutely filled with buildings dedicated to the housing and worship of gods. But the first Christians didn't have big buildings to worship in. For them, church wasn't about a specific place or shrine or monument. Church was about *people*.

The word *church* came from the Greek term *ekklesia*. It means "an assembly of citizens"—a people called together for a purpose. Among the Christians, "church" meant the gathered bunch of believers in a certain city or town. When an ancient Christian wrote a letter to a church, or went to visit one, they were thinking not about a building but about a specific group of people claimed by Jesus and united through baptism.

Since "church" meant a group of people and not a building, Christian churches could be anywhere. Christians gathered together in all kinds of places, including homes, shops, gardens, and fields.

## Similar to the Synagogue

By the time of Jesus, Jews had been meeting together in synagogues to pray, study the Bible, and conduct community business for many years. *Synagogue* is a Greek word that means "a gathering of people," but it also refers to the place where those people gather. Synagogues were typically the centers of Jewish communities all over the empire. Nearly every city of any size had a synagogue or two. They were used as schools, for communal meals, as accommodations for guests, as law courts, and as a place to give or receive charity. Most of the synagogues of this time were large halls with benches around the outer edge of the room. Because almost all of the first Christians were also Jews, their experience of synagogue life and worship helped shape the early Christian church communities.

## House Church

The oldest recognizably Christian place of worship that archaeologists have found is a small house in the Roman fortress town of Dura-Europos in what is now Syria. The whole town was abandoned when the Persians threatened to invade the city in the year 256. One modestly sized house had been converted into a space for Christian worship. The owners had knocked down two interior walls to make a room large enough for the whole community to gather for reading, preaching, and singing—and of course the Eucharist meal, which was the central part of Sunday worship.

The Christians of Dura-Europos also built a smaller room with a stone tub for baptisms. The walls in the baptistery were painted with scenes and images from the Bible—especially the life of Jesus. The picture placed right over the baptismal font was Jesus as the Good Shepherd, carrying a lost sheep on his shoulders. Church, for these Christians, was the flock of lost lambs, safely gathered by Jesus.

# DAILY BREAD

For the Christians, bread was part of everyday life. They gave thanks to God for daily bread and shared what they had with each other, as well as with their poorer neighbors. Bread was also central to their most important ritual: the holy meal at the heart of the Eucharist, where bread symbolized Jesus' body. And bread was important to everyone else in the Roman world as well—nearly every meal in ancient Rome would have included warm, leavened bread.

## Wheat or Weeds?

Roman bread was made from a wide variety of grains. The most common were barley and bread wheat, but grains like spelt and even lentils made their way into loaves. Bakers also added honey and oil and dried fruits to their products. The tastiest and most expensive loaves used finely ground wheat flour and were sweetened with honey and oil. The city of Rome, with its taste for these finer things, had to import all its wheat from elsewhere. The provinces of Egypt and Sicily were the main suppliers of wheat for the whole empire.

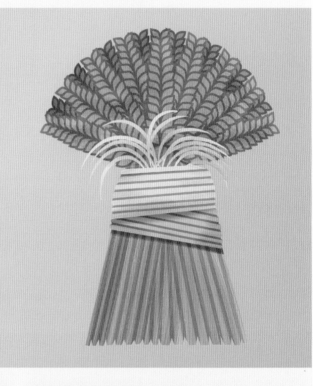

## The Oven

The oven had a flat floor, often made of granite or lava rock. To heat it up, the chamber was filled with wood and the wood was lit. After it burned down to embers, the ashes were pushed into a pile and the loaves shoveled in with a paddle. Larger, bi-level ovens had a top shelf for the loaves and a bottom area for continual fire. Thin breads went in first, then large round loaves. After an hour or so, these were pulled out and replaced by more delicate pastries, which needed less heat to bake.

## The Loaf

This common round loaf of bread, called *panis quadratus*, could be easily broken into pieces for sharing around the table. Ancient bakers likely made the marks using a small, wooden wagon wheel.

## Mill for Grinding Grain into Bread Flour

Bakeries often had an area for grinding flour, with four or more mills, called *molina*. The upper, funnel-shaped stone moved around the lower grindstone. Flour fell through the mill, collecting on lead sheets atop the mill's base. Donkeys or slaves walked in circles moving the millstone for hours and hours every day. Flour made in this way often included a little bit of ground-up stone (and probably some sweat) as well as grain.

## Bread Stamps

Some bakers added a personal flourish to the loaves they produced, or decorated ceremonial bread with pictures or symbols of gods and heroes. Bronze or clay bread stamps with an image or letters were pressed onto the soft dough. As the bread baked, the stamped image became part of the finished product. In community ovens, a stamp or signature would let everyone know whose loaf belonged to whom. For larger, commercial bakeries it was also a point of pride and a legal thing. Bread was regulated by Roman laws, and everything from cost to ingredients to loaf size was controlled. Selling too-small loaves, or bread with fillers like sawdust baked in, could get the baker in serious trouble.

## The Bakers

The men who ran the commercial bakeries in Roman cities were powerful and influential people. If they got the contract to supply bread to the people on behalf of the government, they could also become very wealthy. Baking daily bread for an entire city required massive quantities of wheat and other grains, fresh water, firewood, and countless hours of slave and animal labor. The biggest bakeries in the largest cities turned out thousands of loaves every day.

# THE EMPEROR

For most of its history, Rome was ruled by emperors. Emperors were at the top of Roman society in every way, with every other person in the known world beneath them, expected to serve the emperor and even worship him as a god on earth.

• • • • • •

Between the time of Jesus and the chaotic start of the fourth century, Rome saw more than fifty emperors claim or attempt to claim control of the empire. The longest reign belonged to Augustus, who ruled for forty years. The shortest time in office was that of Gordian I and his son, Gordian II, who shared the hot seat for just twenty-one days. The eighty or so years between the rise of Emperor Trajan and the death of Marcus Aurelius were a period of stability and prosperity in the empire, with only four different emperors. In contrast, the fifty years between 235 and 285 AD saw more than twenty-five rulers come and go; all but one died a violent death.

• • • • • •

Just one woman was named empress of Rome. In September of the year 275, Ulpia Severina, the widow of Emperor Aurelian, stepped into her late husband's place. Taking the title *Pia Augusta*, she ruled very briefly before the election of Emperor Tacitus.

Because almost everybody used (or wanted to use) coins, they became a great place for rulers to put messages and symbols—including their names and accomplishments. Knowing that money would move throughout the empire and find its way into all kinds of hands, emperors had their faces and titles, as well as symbols of Rome's greatness, stamped on the surfaces of gold, silver, copper, and brass coins.

It wasn't the temples that gave the emperor his unbelievable power; it was the military troops. Smart emperors kept the troops happy, well fed, and financially supported. Rulers who ignored or abused the military, or who failed to keep the respect of the guys with the swords, didn't last long.

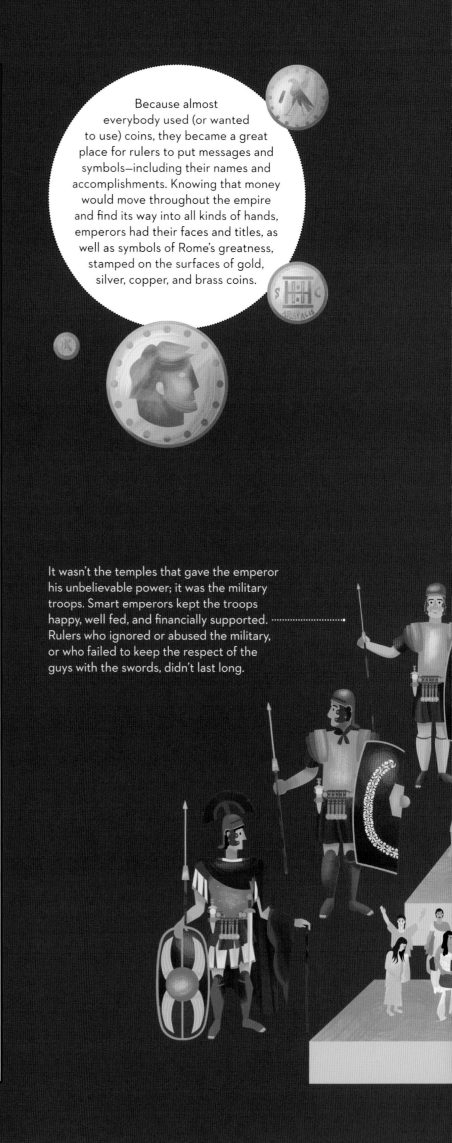

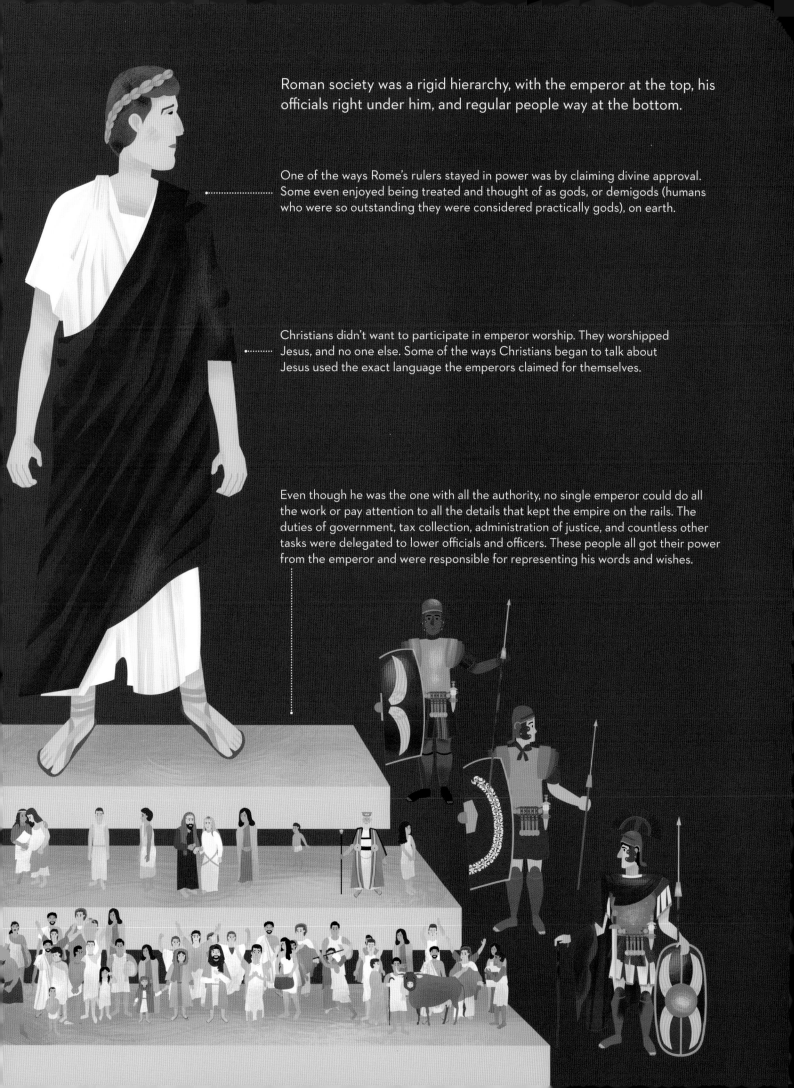

Roman society was a rigid hierarchy, with the emperor at the top, his officials right under him, and regular people way at the bottom.

One of the ways Rome's rulers stayed in power was by claiming divine approval. Some even enjoyed being treated and thought of as gods, or demigods (humans who were so outstanding they were considered practically gods), on earth.

Christians didn't want to participate in emperor worship. They worshipped Jesus, and no one else. Some of the ways Christians began to talk about Jesus used the exact language the emperors claimed for themselves.

Even though he was the one with all the authority, no single emperor could do all the work or pay attention to all the details that kept the empire on the rails. The duties of government, tax collection, administration of justice, and countless other tasks were delegated to lower officials and officers. These people all got their power from the emperor and were responsible for representing his words and wishes.

# DIVIDING UP THE WORLD

The Roman world maintained rigid distinctions between different types and classes of people. In the cities of the empire, one could usually see at a glance whether a person was rich or poor, slave or free, Jew or Greek, citizen or not. Christianity was radical in that it didn't observe these distinctions. Christians were found at all levels of society and came from every ethnic background. In this sense, Christianity was both inclusive and universal—everyone was welcome.

Jews covered their heads and wore the clothing prescribed by their religious laws, including a fringed cloak. Jewish men wore beards, unlike most Romans.

## Roman Citizens

Part of what made the Roman Empire work was the way it incorporated the people and cultures it conquered and absorbed them into the empire. From the point of view of the empire, a person's ethnicity or birthplace was less important than their status.

Status was everything. Every person had their place in society, from the most honored and exalted emperor at the top to the most worthless and wretched slave at the bottom. According to this worldview, the basic line of division was between those who were free and those who were enslaved. Free people belonged to themselves; slaves belonged to somebody else.

The toga was a symbol of Roman citizenship. No foreigner was allowe to wear the toga.

## Jewish People

Being Jewish was (and for many people still is today) a whole-life identity including religion, ethnicity, and tradition. Jewish people trace their ancestry back to Abraham, whose family was chosen by God to be a blessing to other nations. The Jewish religion and culture were based on this promise and on the covenant relationship between God and the Jewish people. The Jewish people referred to non-Jews as *goyim*, which in Hebrew means "the nations" or "the peoples." The English word for this is "gentile."

Women of all classes wore more clothing than men— usually a robe or dress that covered their legs.

## Slaves

Just like in more modern times, slavery was a degrading and brutal institution that treated people as property. One Latin term for an enslaved person was "a tool that speaks."

At the height of the Roman Empire, about one out of every four people was enslaved. The percentage was higher in the big cities. Slaves were everywhere. They worked in mines and factories, in wealthy households, and on farms. Public slaves worked for city governments, building roads, aqueducts, and buildings. The empire could not have functioned without the unpaid labor of millions of slaves.

Working-class and poor people typically wore a simple tunic and sandals.

Some slaves were given wooden shoes.

Kids wore loose tunics, or whatever was available. Children, even if they weren't slaves, were vulnerable members of Roman society.

## A NEW THING AMONG THE CHRISTIANS

The message about Jesus included a radical shift in thinking about differences between people. Rather than identifying whom to exclude, Christianity included people of every category. Jesus was a savior for everybody, and all people were believed to be children of God. Baptism welcomed slave and free, young and old, rich and poor, male and female into a relationship and a community that strove to erase the ways ancient people divided up the world. The church that gathered around the story and example of Jesus was a place where the old divisions didn't get the final word. In Christ, there is a new creation, and a new way of being human together.

This part of the Christian message, and the way it shaped how the first Christians viewed and treated one another and their neighbors, was attractive to many, but it was confusing or threatening to others because it challenged the ways people were accustomed to seeing the world. The Christians' countercultural willingness to welcome and serve people from all backgrounds and social statuses helped the church grow in exciting, and sometimes unexpected, ways.

# FROM SCROLL...

In all the many centuries before the development of the printing press, books were written by hand. As of the beginning of the first century AD, the papyrus scroll was the preferred format for letters and for books of all types. But within a hundred years or so, a new format started to grow in popularity.

Scrolls were usually rolled around a wooden rod. To read the book, you unrolled the scroll from one side and rewound it on the other side as you went along. A rolled-up scroll was called a *volumen* in Latin. We get the book-word volume from this.

The *titulus* attached to the scroll indicated the book's contents. English gets the book-word title from this tag. The Greek word for the scroll's label was *sillybos*.

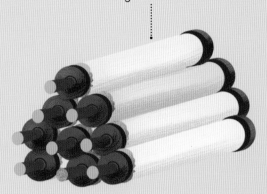

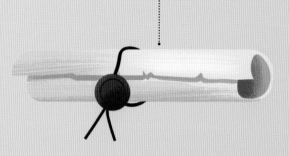

Wooden knobs topped the rods on which the scrolls were rolled up. These knobs were known as *capites*, or "heads." Long works that took up several scrolls were said to have many heads. The English word *chapter* comes from this word.

- The Bible's book of Isaiah required several scrolls because it was so long.

- Scrolls were usually stored stacked in deep shelves, or tucked into pigeonholes. Special, rare, or valuable scrolls were stored in boxes.

- Ancient libraries in Alexandria, Ephesus, Pergamum, and Rome held thousands and thousands of scrolls.

## People of the Book

Unlike most of the other religions at the time, Judaism and Christianity had sacred scriptures at the heart of the faith. For believers, reading, discussing, studying, and commenting on the words of their holy books was a central part of worship and community life. Over time, and for all kinds of reasons, Christians began to prefer the codex over the scroll.

# ...TO CODEX

The invention of the codex, which transformed books from one long piece of material into a pile of pages collected between covers, changed the way people wrote, read, and thought about how books could be used. It took a couple hundred years, but the codex went on to almost completely replace the scroll. Today, it's the thing we imagine whenever anybody says "book."

Codexes were constructed by beginning with sheets of papyrus or parchment—as many as you needed for what you were writing. Even after you put together your codex, you could take it apart and add more pages if you needed to.

Next, the sheets would be sewn together.

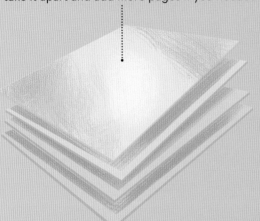

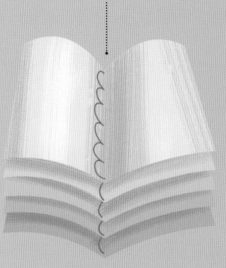

Ultimately, the codex would be given a cover made of wood. This is what gave codexes their name—the word in Latin refers to tree trunks. Eventually, these covers were embellished with stamps or designs.

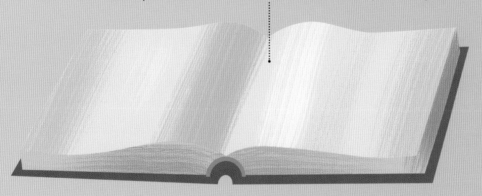

## Some Advantages of the Codex:
- Easy to search: turn pages to find what you're looking for.
- Can add page numbers.
- Can lie flat while open.
- Cheaper: can write on both sides of the page.
- Easier to shelve and organize: title can be written on the spine.
- Can add or remove pages to make a collection.

# THE CRUCIFIED GOD

In the ancient world, crucifixion was considered one of the most brutal and shameful modes of death. As a way of humiliating, torturing, and killing enemies, it probably originated among the armies of the Assyrian and Babylonian Empires. The Persians used it throughout the sixth century BC. Alexander the Great of Greece learned crucifixion from the Persians, used it often, and introduced the practice to the eastern part of the Mediterranean in the fourth century BC. The Phoenicians introduced it to Rome in the third century BC.

As they did with most inventions and techniques that came from the cultures absorbed by their expansion, the Romans took what they learned about crucifixion and ran with it, perfecting and innovating on the basics for the next five hundred years, until the fourth century AD. In Roman times, crucifixion was a punishment reserved for slaves, disgraced soldiers, traitors to the state (including Christians), and foreigners convicted of crimes.

According to army policy on executions, attending Roman guards could only leave a crucifixion site after the victim had died. Antsy or bored guards were known to speed up death by breaking the victim's legs with a mallet or club, stabbing them in the heart with a spear, beating on their chest, or lighting a smoky fire under the cross. With the pain and suffering the process entailed, it's not hard to understand how English gets the word *excruciating*, which means "out of the cross."

For ancient people, the cross was absolutely disgusting and utterly bad news. Crosses were for losers in battle, defeated enemies, rebellious slaves, and vicious criminals. Crucifixion was a punishment reserved for the worst offenders, people who deserved only ridicule and contempt.

## Alexamenos Worships His God

This scrawled piece of graffiti from around the year 200 AD, of a man saluting a crucified figure with a donkey's head, seems intended to ridicule the Christians. It's one of a very few ancient images of crucifixion that survive and is an indication of how stupid some Romans thought the Christians were.

The idea of the Son of God being crucified was difficult for ancient people to understand. Early Christians had to rethink their assumptions about God's power and the way God saves. Among the Christians, the awful cross the Romans used to kill Jesus became a sign that revealed who God was and what God was willing to do to save the world. Each of the four gospel accounts of Jesus' life includes the story of his crucifixion. In Christian thought, the cross was transformed from an evil thing to a sign of God's goodness. Christians clung to the hope at the heart of this symbol: that the purpose of Jesus' coming was to save and redeem the whole human race. God's raising of the crucified Jesus was the dawn of a new age in which death, and all its terrible force, wouldn't get the last word.

## The Horrible Process

After a person was convicted and stripped naked, crucifixion started with a severe beating. This was followed by the dazed and bleeding victim being tied or nailed to a cross of wood. It was awful, and bloody, and involved the convicted victim slowly suffocating to death as his or her ravaged and abused body stopped being able to support its own weight. People were nailed to trees or posts or boards, sometimes through hands or arms and feet, and sometimes through other body parts.

## CRUCIFIXION IN THE ANCIENT WORLD

- Alexander the Great reportedly crucified 2,000 survivors from his siege of the Phoenician city of Tyre in 332 BC.

- The Jewish king Alexander Jannaeus, king of Judea from 103 to 76 BC, crucified 800 rebels, said to be Pharisees, in the middle of Jerusalem.

- In ancient Carthage, North Africa, crucifixion was an established mode of execution that could even be inflicted on their own generals who suffered a major defeat.

- Mass crucifixions followed the slave uprising of 73-71 BC in Rome. After defeating 6,000 of the slave leader Spartacus's followers in battle, General Crassus crucified them along the Appian Way.

- In the siege that led to the destruction of Jerusalem in 70 AD, the ancient historian Josephus wrote that the Roman soldiers crucified Jewish captives outside the walls of Jerusalem and, "out of anger and hatred, amused themselves by nailing them in different positions."

- Crucifixion was at last outlawed as a legal punishment in the Roman Empire in the year 337 AD by Constantine the Great, out of reverence for Jesus, its most famous victim.

# THE FIRST CHRISTIAN MARTYRS

For centuries, the Christian religion was illegal in the Roman Empire. Though some emperors and governors tolerated or ignored the Christians, others brutally persecuted and even killed them. By the time of Rome's official announcement of tolerance for Christianity in the year 313, thousands of women and men across the empire had chosen to give up their lives rather than deny Jesus. These people were called *martyrs*.

In dying for their faith, the martyrs were seen as following the way and example of Jesus, who gave his life on the cross. In this way, death was a kind of resistance against powerful rulers who used it to frighten and control people. Jesus' resurrection, and his promise of eternal life to all who believed, robbed death of its power. The martyrs were witnesses to this central truth of the faith.

Some martyrs died in the arena. They might have died by forced combat with gladiators, or with wild animals like lions or bears—this was called *damnatio ad bestias*, or "condemnation to the beasts." Other martyrs were burned at the stake or boiled with oil, among other horrifying methods of death.

> *"The blood of the martyrs is the seed of the church."*
>
> —Tertullian, North Africa

• • • • • • • • • • • • • • • • • • • • • • • • •

The martyrs' heroic stories usually involved their courage and calm throughout awful torture and gruesome death. This inspired and encouraged Christians everywhere to stand fast, even in the face of threats and violence. Martyr stories were told and retold, and martyrs' graves became places that later Christians visited and revered.

Saint Sebastian, killed during the reign of Diocletian, provides one of the most iconic images of martyrs. Legend holds that Sebastian was tied to a post, then shot with arrows.

## NOT JUST CHRISTIANS

Christian martyrdom had its roots in the traditions of Judaism and the witness of the Hebrew scriptures. For centuries before Jesus, Jews had been persecuted and killed—even crucified by various occupying and conquering rulers for publicly declaring and demonstrating their faith. This continued during the first century, especially during and after the Jewish revolt of 66-70 AD, which included the destruction of Jerusalem and its temple.

## SAINT STEPHEN
### The First Martyr

According to the Bible, the first martyr was Stephen, a deacon of the brand-new Jerusalem church. Around the year 34 AD, Stephen provoked the anger of the city's synagogue leadership, who put him on trial for blasphemy against God's name. He responded to his accusers with a long speech denouncing his judges and praising Christ as the fulfillment of all God's promises. He was stoned to death by the furious crowd, even as he asked God to forgive them. Read the story, and his epic sermon, in Acts 7.

## PUTTING THE WIT IN WITNESSES

Some martyr stories include touches of humor, showing the assurance and steadfastness of the martyr at the expense of their torturers. One story about a young deacon named Lawrence, who was condemned to death by being roasted over a fire, includes him telling his murderers, "You can turn me over now—I am done on that side."

# A PEOPLE OF MERCY

The first Christians were a busy bunch. In addition to praying and preaching, the people who flowed into the world after Jesus' resurrection went looking for people who were hurting so they could help. Following Jesus' command to "love your neighbor as yourself," these early Christians saw the suffering of others as an opportunity to provide care in Jesus' name.

## Burying the Dead

In the ancient world, it was not guaranteed that one would be buried after death. Many people worried about who would care for their remains when they died. Not only did Christians bury their own dead, but they often looked after the funeral needs of strangers and poor people who died alone.

Not being afraid of death made quite a difference for the early Christians. Christianity offered the believer a life beyond death, free from sickness, poverty, and loneliness. Christians took comfort and courage from these promises. Their faith often made them less afraid to do things such as help victims of plague, give away food and possessions, and care for strangers.

*"Whenever you do this for them, you're doing it for me."* —Jesus

## Caring for the Sick and Dying

There were no public hospitals in the ancient world. While the wealthy could afford to hire a physician, most people had no access to any kind of care and were at the mercy of home remedies or magic. Part of Christianity's appeal was as a healing religion. Jesus was known as a healer, and his disciples had a reputation for miracles of this kind as well. Even when they had no miracles to offer, Christians looked after the needs of the sick, sometimes nursing people abandoned by their families back to health. Especially in times of mass illness and plagues, which swept through Rome's cities from time to time, the basic care offered by Christians helped many sick people survive.

### The Image of God

Christians and Jews shared the belief that human beings were made in God's image. This gave each human life a value that wasn't recognized by many other religions or philosophies in the ancient world.

## Visiting Prisoners

Christians visited prisons, bringing food, water, and company to those who were cut off from their families. For Christian prisoners, they prayed and offered encouragement. For non-Christians they prayed and shared the gospel. Sometimes they made a point of asking the guards to treat the prisoners well or of arguing for their release.

## Feeding the Hungry

The church appointed deacons to be servant-leaders whose job was distributing food and help to the poorest members of the community, including local widows and orphans—anyone without the protection of family. After worship services, the deacons and others would bring extra bread to people in need.

# FIRE IN ROME 64 AD

On the 19th of July, in the tenth year of the Emperor Nero's reign, a fire started in one of Rome's huge stadiums, known as the Circus Maximus. The fire got out of control and burned for more than six days, destroying almost three-quarters of the city. It was a mess. Many of the city's buildings were large, poorly constructed, wood and brick apartment buildings. They burned fast and hot. Many people died, and the destruction was terrible.

### An Awful Emperor

In the early years of his reign, Nero could be a responsible and generous ruler. At some point, however, he realized that, as emperor, he could really do whatever he wanted. In addition to erecting a colossal statue of himself in the center of Rome, Nero had both his mother and his wife assassinated. He was also the first emperor to order the persecution of Christians in the capital city, and his cruelty toward them is legendary.

Although he ended up being a selfish and often brutal ruler, the legend of Nero sitting around playing the lyre while the city burned is probably not true. Regardless, history wasn't kind; after his death by suicide, the Senate damned his memory and knocked the face off his colossal statue.

## Roman Revenge

Christians as well as Jews were swept up in the aftermath of the fire. To incite the opinion of the people of Rome against them, Nero called the Christians "haters of humanity" and denounced them as dangerous traitors. He ordered them to be tortured and killed in all kinds of horrible ways. Some were crucified while others were torn apart by dogs. Some poor people were smeared with tar and lit on fire as human torches—payback for the crime they were accused of. At the time, some Romans had compassion for the Christians, seeing them as unfortunate victims of Nero's cruelty.

Even before the fire was out, a rumor circulated that the unpopular emperor Nero had the fire started because he wanted to build a grand new palace for himself in the center of Rome. Worried about unrest and riots, Nero decided to blame the fire on a small and strange new sect of not-quite-Jews in town: the Christians.

This event marked the first time the Roman higher-ups officially recognized a difference between Jews and Christians. Most Romans, if they had heard anything about Christians at all, didn't much care about the differences between the two groups. Everybody was angry and scared, and somebody was going to get blamed. The small community of Roman Christians became the scapegoats.

It was most likely during this period of anti-Christian violence and hatred that the apostles Peter and Paul were executed, along with an unknown number of Roman Christians and Jews.

## So, Who Started the Fire?

Although ancient historians with an axe to grind blamed Nero, it almost certainly wasn't him. An emperor had the power to simply take property and have it cleared away if he wanted to. It also wasn't the Christians. Most likely, the fire was an accident, started from an oil lamp or some other source. Once the fire grew, Rome's poorly built wooden structures just kept burning. The city's small crew of mostly slave firefighters and watchmen had no chance.

From the ruins of this catastrophic fire, Rome was rebuilt as a Greek-style city of gleaming marble, wide streets, flowing fountains, and open spaces. Wanting to prevent future disasters, Nero also ordered improvements to the fire department and improved the city's water supplies.

# THE CATACOMBS

People in every era and culture have had to decide what to do with their dead. Some choices made throughout history have included practices like burial, cremation, and mummification. All these options were in play during the centuries of the Roman Empire, usually based on the traditions and beliefs of the people involved. Romans often preferred cremation and storage of the bones and ashes. Egyptians had been making mummies for millennia. Believing that God would resurrect their bodies, Christians buried their dead. Regardless of the specific way they treated their departed loved ones, nearly everyone in the ancient world took this part of life very seriously.

Roman law had a lot to say about dealing with the dead. This had to do with sanitation and keeping huge cities free of disease, but it was also because Romans were superstitious about ghosts and the spirits of offended ancestors. It was a law that nobody could be buried inside a city's walls. Tombs, columbaria, mausoleums, and cemeteries had to be built on the outskirts of town, among the hills and along the roads surrounding the city. This is where the first catacombs were dug, as places for Jews and, later, for Christians to be buried with their sisters and brothers in the faith.

Palms were a Roman symbol of victory. Among the Christians, they were carved onto tombs to proclaim Jesus' victory over death for the faithful departed.

This woman's gravestone was inscribed with her picture and name (Severa), and the Christian hope in which she rests: "In God she lives."

SEVERA IN DEO VI VAS

A *catacomb* is an underground system of tunnels and chambers built for the purpose of burying lots of people in a limited amount of space.

## Dark Down There

The light from above could get pretty weak, especially in the lower levels of a big catacomb. Clay lamps that burned olive oil offered illumination. Sometimes these lamps were cemented onto the gravestone, near the deceased's head. Visitors brought new oil for these lamps and left the light burning when they went home.

Often the deceased would be shown at worship, standing in the common prayer position called *orans*. Christians didn't start praying on their knees for several more centuries.

Catacombs were often located under farm fields or orchards.

Carved into the soft rock of the walls in nearly every space were wide, shallow shelves for the dead. These shelves, or niches, were called *loculi*. A *loculus* was just the right size for a lying-down human body to fit.

## Goddess of the Ghosts

The Roman goddess Trivia was believed to haunt crossroads and graveyards. She was the protector of the entry points between the worlds of the dead and the living. Many Romans believed that dogs could see this goddess and that their barking announced that she was near.

## Asleep in God

Christians believed that death was a kind of sleep, in which the departed lay waiting to be awakened by Jesus' call on the last day of history. They looked forward to reuniting with their loved ones.

## Don't Mess with My Bones

The fear of having one's grave disturbed or one's remains scattered was a big thing; Rome even had ancient laws that declared burial grounds sacred places. Grave robbery, called "tomb-breaking," could be punished by death. Because cemetery space was limited, especially near larger cities, moving someone's remains and using their tomb was not uncommon, even if it was illegal.

## Dining with the Dead

A common Roman practice, shared by the Christians, was the family celebration of a loved one's death day. The church would gather at the grave on the anniversary of a member's death to celebrate a ritual meal, which often included the Eucharist. Some graves even had little holes in the covering stone so a little wine could be shared with the deceased sister or brother.

# THE MONKS OF EGYPT

Around the year 270, in a small town in Egypt, a young Christian man named Anthony stepped into church and heard a reading from the Gospel of Matthew. In the passage, Jesus answers another young man who asks what he must do to inherit eternal life by saying this: "If you want to be perfect, go, sell your possessions and give to the poor, and you will have treasure in heaven. Then come, follow me" (19:21). Anthony heard Jesus' words as being spoken directly to him, and apparently had a revelation about the purpose of his life. He walked out of the worship service and walked into history. Anthony of Egypt is known as the father of Christian monasticism.

### Desert Mothers
Although most of the people who took up the hard and dangerous life of a hermit were men, who enjoyed more freedom than women did to choose their own path in the ancient world, some of the first monks were women. They offered the same kind of leadership and spiritual wisdom as their brother monks, and many were honored with the title *Amma*, which means "mother." One of the greatest was Amma Theodora, who said, "Neither exercise and self-denial, nor vigils, nor any kind of suffering are able to save. Only true humility can do that."

## There Were Others Out There
The story of Anthony says that he met an even older monk already out there in the desert. This man's name was Paul, and legend has it that he was fed by ravens like the prophet Elijah. Each day, a bird would bring him bread. Paul also was said to have a pet lion. As well as Paul and his beasts, historians believe there were communities of Jewish hermits in the deserts of Egypt as early as the time of Jesus. Legend also claims John the Baptist as the first Christian monk, and the pioneer of the monastic way of life.

Anthony's parents had died a few months earlier, so he sold his family's home and farm and all their possessions. With nothing but the clothes on his back, Anthony walked out of town to pursue a life of prayer, simple work, and struggle to follow the teachings and example of Jesus. For a dozen years or so, he made his home among the tombs at the edge of town, receiving visitors who sought his wisdom or asked for prayer and healing. Then, looking for even more isolation, Anthony moved farther out, beyond the fertile green land beside the Nile, into the desolate Egyptian desert.

Anthony and all who followed in his footsteps attempted to live lives of devotion to God, free from self-indulgence and marked by self-denial, generosity, and spiritual exercise. Male and female monks sought simple holiness, which they understood was to be found beyond the day-to-day distractions that come with village or city life—and beyond the reach of the empire's interference. This model of life, with its disciplines of prayer and fasting and withdrawal from the regular activities of society, has endured throughout the centuries as Christian monks and nuns follow in the early monks' path.

### Work and Prayer
In addition to spending hours in prayer and wrestling with demonic temptations, the monks worked, often weaving palm fronds into mats and baskets and sandals, which they traded in the villages for food and water, or gave away to people in need. The monks also ate the sugary dates from the palms, which grew in the marshy oases of the desert.

# BIOS

**Marc Olson** lives and works in Saint Paul, MN. He studied theology and theatre. As well as working as an educator, bus driver, garbage hauler, and undertaker, Marc has served as a Lutheran pastor. His favorite part of that job was teaching kids and adults, and writing and preaching.

**Jemima Maybank** is an illustrator living in Leeds, England, who is fascinated by the ancient Orthodox icons of saints found in many cathedrals of the UK. In her free time she likes running and trying to stop her houseboat from sinking.